Albert B. Simpson

The Four-Fold Gospel

Third Edition

Albert B. Simpson

The Four-Fold Gospel
Third Edition

ISBN/EAN: 9783337285128

Printed in Europe, USA, Canada, Australia, Japan

Cover: Foto ©Lupo / pixelio.de

More available books at **www.hansebooks.com**

THE
FOUR-FOLD GOSPEL

BY

REV. A. B. SIMPSON

THIRD EDITION, REVISED

PUBLISHED BY
THE CHRISTIAN ALLIANCE PUBLISHING CO.
692 EIGHTH AVENUE, NEW YORK

THE
Four-Fold Gospel.

CONTENTS.

I.
CHRIST OUR SAVIOUR, - - 7

II.
CHRIST OUR SANCTIFIER, 42

III.
CHRIST OUR HEALER, 75

IV.
CHRIST OUR COMING LORD, 110

I.

CHRIST OUR SAVIOUR.

And they cried with a loud voice, saying, salvation to our God which sitteth upon the throne, and unto the Lamb. Rev. vii : 10.

THIS is the cry of the ransomed around the throne when the universe is dissolving in wreck, and terror is filling the hearts of men. It is the first cry of the ransomed after they reach their home and have seen all that it means to be lost and to be saved, while the earth is reeling, and the elements are melting, and all things are quaking and trembling in the first approaches of the great catastrophe. They see behind them all the way through which the Lord has led them; down that long vista they behold the toils they have come through and the perils they have escaped, and they recognize how tenderly the grace of God has led them on and kept them safe. They see the robes and crowns that are prepared for them, and all the joy of the eternal future which is opening before them. They see all this, and then they behold Him whose hand has kept it all safely for them, and whose heart has chosen it for them. They look back upon all the past: they look forward into all the future;

they look up into the face of Him to whom it was all due, and then they lift up their voices in one glad exultant cry, "Salvation to our God which sitteth upon the throne, and unto the Lamb." This is what salvation means; this is what they have believed for; this is what He died to give them. They have it all. They are saved, and the full realization of it has come home to their heart at last.

Let us look a little at what it means to be saved. It is not at all a little thing. We sometimes hear that certain Christians are *only* justified. It is a mighty thing to be justified. It is a glorious thing to be born again. Christ said it was greater to have one's name written in heaven than to be able to cast out devils. What does salvation mean?

I. WHAT IT SAVES US FROM.

1. It takes away the guilt of sin. It frees us from all liability and punishment for past offences. Sin deserves punishment. Salvation takes this all away. Is it not glorious to be saved?

2. Salvation saves us from the wrath of God. God hates evil and must punish it somehow. The wrath of God is revealed from heaven against all unrighteousness of men. But from this salvation delivers us.

3. Salvation delivers us from the curse of the law. We can recall the

terrors of its revealing, the lightnings and thunder that surrounded the mountain, and the terror of Israel before it was given at all. They could not bear that God should speak to them thus, and they entreated Moses, "Speak thou with us and we will hear; but let not God speak with us, lest we die." But if the giving of the law was terrible, more terrible was the breaking. It is perilous to break the law of the land. The most tender appeal of affection did not avail to save those condemned anarchists in Chicago recently. The hand of the law was on their throats, and to the gallows they must go. I remember the days when the assassin of President Lincoln was stalking through the land. The law would have searched the world to find him out. How terrible it must have been for him to feel that the eye of justice was looking for him, and sooner or later would surely find him! The circle narrowed and narrowed around him, till at last he was grasped in the cordon. So the cordon of law tightens around the sinner who is under its power. Salvation delivers us from this curse through Him who was made a curse for us.

4. It delivers us also from our evil conscience. There is always a shadow left on our hearts by sin, and a feeling of remorse. It is the black wing of the raven, and its hoarse voice is

ever whispering of despair. The memory of past guilt will follow people so that after many years they tell of crimes committed, the punishment for which they escaped, but the burden never left their conscience. Sometimes it seemed to slumber for a while, and at last it sprang upon them like a lion. Salvation delivers from our evil conscience. It takes the shadow from the heart and the stinging memory of sin from the soul.

5. It delivers from an evil heart, which is the source of all the sin in the life. It is natural for men to sin even while they hate it. The tendency to evil is in every nature, chained to it like a body of death,

so that when we would do good evil is present with us. It takes possession of the will and heart, like a living death. It is offensive, it smells of the sepulchre, it is full of the poison of asps, it putrefies the whole moral being and bears it, too, down to death. Salvation frees us from its power and gives us a new nature.

6. It frees us from the fear of death. It takes away the sting of that last enemy, through fear of whom we would otherwise all our lifetime be subject to bondage. I remember when I was a child what a shock a funeral bell would give me. I could not bear to hear of some one's being dead. The love of Christ has taken this all away. The

death-bed of God's children is to them the portal of heaven.

7. Salvation delivers us from Satan's power and kingdom. God hath "delivered us from the power of darkness and translated us into the kingdom of His dear Son." We are saved from the ills and the serpent and the bonds of sin, and the devil is for us a conquered foe. Salvation delivers us from much sorrow and distress in life. It brings a glorious sunlight into the life and drives away those clouds of depression and gloom which overwhelm us.

8. Beyond all else, salvation delivers us from eternal death. We are not going down into outer dark-

ness and the depths of woe. Christ has unlocked the fetters of the pit and saved us from endless death. We are delivered from that terrible agony which the kindest lips that ever spoke has called "the worm that dieth not and the fire that is not quenched."

These are some of the things that salvation has delivered us from. Is it not indeed glad tidings?

II. WHAT SALVATION BRINGS TO US.

1. It brings the forgiveness of all our sins and entirely removes them. They are blotted out as completely as though we had paid all that was due for them, and they can never appear against us again.

2. It brings us justification in the sight of God, so that we stand before Him as righteous beings. We are accepted as though we had done everything He had commanded, and had perfectly kept the law in every particular. With one stroke of the pen He erases the account that was against us; with another stroke He puts there all the righteousness of Christ. We must take both sides of this. The spotlessness of Jesus is put to your account as if it were your own. All His obedience to the Father is yours. All His patience and gentleness are yours. Every service that He has rendered to bless others is put to your account as if you had done it all. Every good

18   THE FOUR-FOLD GOSPEL.

thing you can discover in Him is yours, and every evil thing in you is His. That is salvation. Is it not wonderful?

3. It brings us into the favor and love of God, and secures us full acceptance in the person of Jesus. He loves us as He loves His only begotten Son. The moment we are presented in the arms of Christ, we are accepted in Him. Dr. Currie, a brilliant writer connected with the Methodist Episcopal Church, has left a beautiful incident in his own life. He was the editor of one of the best journals of his church, and in many ways he was closely connected with its work. He dreamed one night, a little before his recent death, that he

died and went up to the gate of heaven. There he met an angel and asked to be allowed to enter. The angel asked him who he was. He answered: "I am Dr. Currie, the editor of the *Quarterly Review* of the Methodist Episcopal Church." The angel answered: "I don't know you, I never heard of you before." Soon he met another angel and told him the same story, and received the same answer: "I don't know you." At last one of the angels said: "Let us go to the Judge and see if He will know you." He went before the throne and told the Judge about his life and the work he had done for the church, but received the answer from the Judge: "I don't know you at all." His heart was beginning to gather the blackness of despair, when suddenly there was One at his side with a crown of thorns upon his head, who said: "Father, I know him. I will answer for him." And instantly all the harps of heaven began to sing: "Worthy is the Lamb that was slain," and he was ushered into all the glory of the celestial world. Not all the preaching we have done, or all the service we have rendered will amount to anything there. We must be identified with the man who wore the thorns; we must be accepted in the Beloved, and then the Father will love us even as He loves His Son. We shall stand with Him even as Christ does.

4. Salvation gives us a new heart. It brings to us regeneration of the soul. Every spark of life from the old polluted nature is worthless, and the divine nature is born in us as a part of our very being.

5. Salvation gives us grace to live day by day. A man may be pardoned and so get out of prison, and yet have no money to supply his needs. He is pardoned, yet he is starving. Salvation takes us out of prison, and provides for all our needs besides. It enables us to rejoice in the glory of God, which is "able to keep us from falling, and to present us faultless before the presence is His glory with exceeding joy."

6. It brings to us the help of the

Holy Spirit, who is ever at our side as a gentle mother, helping our infirmities and bringing grace for every time of need.

7. It brings to us the care of God's providence, causing all things to work together for our good. This is never true until we are saved; but when we are the children of God all things in earth and in heaven are on our side.

8. Salvation opens the way for all the blessings that follow it. It is the stepping stone to sanctification and healing, and the peace that passeth understanding. From this first gateway the prospect opens out boundlessly to all the good land we may go on to possess.

9. Salvation brings us to eternal life. It is, of course, only the beginning, but the heavenly land has its portals open even here, and when we at last reach the throne and look out and see all the possibilities that yet lie before us, we shall sing with the ransomed, "Salvation to our God which sitteth upon the throne, and unto the Lamb."

III. THE PROCESS BY WHICH THESE BLESSINGS COME.

1. They come through the mercy and grace of God. God so loved the world that "He gave His only begotten Son, that whosoever believeth in Him should not perish, but have everlasting life."

2. Salvation comes to us by the righteousness of Jesus Christ. He perfectly fulfilled for us every requirement of the law. Had he faltered in one temptation we could not have been saved. Think of that, when you are tempted to speak a hasty word, and you almost give way for a moment. Suppose Jesus had done so, we should have been lost forever. Every moment He held steadfastly in the path of obedience, and His perfect grace and obedience is the price of your salvation.

3. Salvation comes to us through the death of Christ. His obedience is not enough. He must die. His crucifixion is the atonement for our sins.

4. Salvation comes through the resurrection of Jesus Christ from the dead, which was God's seal of His accomplished work and the pledge of our pardon.

5. Salvation comes through the intercession of Jesus at the right hand of the Father. He is our Great High Priest there, where He ever liveth to make intercession for us, and thus keeps us in continual acceptance.

6. Salvation comes through the grace of the Holy Ghost. The Spirit of God is sent down, through the intercession of Christ, to carry out in our hearts and lives His work. He keeps our feet in the way, and He will never leave His work until He

has put us forever into the bosom of Jesus.

7. Salvation comes to us by the Gospel. It is presented to us through this message, and our refusal to accept it, or our neglect to do so, fixes irrevocably, by our own act, our eternal condition. If we are saved, we become so by accepting the Gospel, which is, therefore, called "the Gospel of your salvation."

IV. THE STEPS BY WHICH IT IS RECEIVED.

1. Conviction of sin. We must first see our need and our danger before we can be saved. The Holy Ghost brings this to our heart and conscience. Until there is this

knowledge of the need of Christ, He cannot of course be received, but when the heart is deeply impressed under a sense of sin, Christ is precious indeed.

2. There must be next an apprehension of Jesus as our Saviour. The soul must see Him as both able and willing to save. It will not do merely to feel and confess your guilt. What is needed is to get the eye on Jesus. So Christ says to every seeking soul, "Look! Look! Look unto me and be saved!" "Every one whick *seeth* the Son, and believeth on Him, may have everlasting life."

3. Salvation comes by repentance. There must be a turning from sin.

This does not consist in mere emotional feeling, necessarily, but it does mean to have the whole will and purpose of heart turned from sin to God.

4. Salvation comes by coming to Jesus. The soul must not only turn away from sin. That alone will not save it. Lot's wife turned away from Sodom — but she was not in Zoar. There must be a turning to Jesus as well as a turning from sin.

5. Salvation comes by accepting Jesus as a Saviour. This does not mean merely crying out to Him to save, but claiming Him as the Saviour, embracing the promises He has given, and so believing that He is your personal Redeemer.

6. Salvation comes by believing that Christ has accepted us, and counting Him faithful who has promised. This will bring the sweetness of assurance and peace, and as we believe the promise the Spirit will seal it to the heart and witness that we are the children of God.

7. Salvation comes by confessing Christ as the Saviour. This is a necessary step. It is like the ratification of a deed or the celebration of a marriage, and stamps and seals our act of committal.

8. Salvation involves our abiding in Jesus. Having taken it for granted, once for all, that you are saved, never do the work over again. "As ye have, therefore, received

Christ Jesus the Lord, so walk ye in Him."

V. THINGS THE BIBLE SAYS ABOUT SALVATION.

1. It is called God's salvation. It was not invented by man. God alone is the author of it, and He is the only Saviour.

2. It is also called "your own salvation," because you yourself must appropriate it.

3. It is called "the common salvation," because it is free to all who will accept it.

4. It is called a "great salvation," because it is full and infinite in its provisions. It is large enough for all your needs.

CHRIST OUR SAVIOUR. 31

5. Christ is called the "mighty to save," because no matter how weak or how wicked the sinner may be, He is able to save him to the uttermost.

6. It is called a near salvation. "Say not in thine heart, who shall ascend into heaven? (that is, to bring Christ down *from above :*) Or, who shall descend into the deep? (that is, to bring Christ again from the dead.) But what saith it? The Word is nigh thee, *even* in thy mouth and in thy heart : that is, the Word of Faith which we preach : That if thou shalt confess with thy mouth the Lord Jesus, and shalt believe in thine heart that God hath raised Him from the dead, thou

shalt be saved." We do not have to get up into some exalted state to find Christ, nor down into some profound and terrible experience, but we can find Him everywhere we are. Salvation is at our door. We can take it as we find Him very near to us. No steps were allowed to God's ancient altar, for then some poor sinner might not be able to get up to it. Jesus is on the very plane where you are this moment. You can take His salvation here now. Take Him as you are, and He will lead you into all the experiences you need.

VI. WHY IT IS CALLED THE GOSPEL OF GOOD NEWS.

1. Because of its value. It comes

laden with blessings to him who receives it.

2. Because of its freedom. It may be taken without money and without price.

3. Because of its availableness. It is easy of access, being on the level of the worst sinner.

4. Because of its universality. Whosoever will may take it and live.

5. Because of the security of its blessings. They are given forevermore. "Verily, verily, I say unto you, He that heareth my Word, and believeth on Him that sent me, hath everlasting life, and shall not perish."

6. Because of the eternity of its

blessings. The sun will have burnt itself into ashes, the earth will have been destroyed by volcanic heat, the heavens will be changed when salvation has only begun. Ten thousand times ten thousand years shall pass away, and we shall have only begun a little to understand what salvation means. Blessed be God for the Gospel of Christ's salvation.

VII. CONSIDERATIONS WHICH SHOULD URGE US TO TAKE AND GIVE OUT THIS SALVATION.

1. Because of the fact that every man's salvation is hinged upon his own choice and free will. It is an awful thing to have the power to take salvation and to throw it away. And yet it is left to our choice. We

are not forced to take it. We must voluntarily choose it or reject it.

2. Because of the tremendous responsibility to which we are held accountable for the salvation of our soul. God has put it into our hands as a jewel of inestimable value, and He will hold us to a strict account for the way we treat this precious thing. If we destroy it, how fearful will be our doom when we meet the Judge of all the earth, and hear the stern question from His lips, "Where is thy soul?"

3. Because of the guilt which will rest upon us for neglecting and despising the precious blood of Christ, which was shed for our salvation. To neglect it is to throw it away. He

has provided a great salvation. If it is worth so much to man, if it has cost God so much to provide it, what can be thought of him who makes little of it? Jesus suffered intensely to bring it to us, and shall we stumble carelessly over it? Oh, let us be more concerned than we are, both for the salvation of our own souls and for those around us who are not saved.

4. Because the little word "now" is always linked with it. It must be taken now or never. The cycle of life is very narrow. We do not know how soon it will end. "Behold now is the day of salvation."

5. Because its issues are for eternity. The decisions there are not

reversible. The soul cannot come back when once it has left the body, and have another chance to secure its salvation. When once the Master has risen up and shut the door, the soul will find it has been left out for ever. The cry will then be, "I have lost my chance ; it is too late." God's Word holds out no second chance to any human soul.

6. Because if salvation is missed there will be no excuse for it. Not one thing has been left undone in presenting it to men. God's best thought and Christ's best love have been given to it. All has been done that could be done. Salvation has been brought down to man's level. It has been placed where he can reach it.

God has provided all the resources, even the grace, repentance and faith, if man will take them. If you lack anything, God will put His arms around you and lift you up to Him, breathing His faith into you, and carrying you Himself until you are able to walk. Salvation is brought to every sinner. If the soul is lost it is because it has neglected and defied God's love.

I am glad to bring you this salvation, but eternity will be too short to tell it all. Take it out and then go out and gather others in to share it. You will receive a glorious crown, but the best of it all will be that men will be saved.

In this city there is a picture hung

up in a parlor and expensively framed. It is a very simple picture. It has just one word on it. On a little bit of paper—a telegraph form—is the one word,

SAVED!

It was framed by the lady of that mansion, and is dearer to her than all her works of art. One day when the awful news came to her through the papers that the ship on which her husband had sailed was a perfect wreck, that little telegram came to her door and saved her from despair.

It came across the sea. It was the message of that rescued man by the electric wire, and it meant to two hearts all that life is worth.

Oh, let such a message go up to-day to yonder shore. The Holy Ghost will flash it hence while I am drawing the next breath. The angels will echo it over heaven, and there are dear friends there to whom it will mean as much as their own very heaven.

I have seen another short sentence in a picture, too.

It came from one who had been rescued from a ship where friends and family had all perished. Those dear little ones were in the slimy caves of the cruel sea. Those beloved faces had gone down forever, but he was saved, and from yonder shore he sent back this sad and weary message,

SAVED ALONE!

So I can imagine a selfish Christian entering yonder portals. They meet him at the gates. "Where are your dear ones?" "Where are your friends?" "Where is your crown?" "Alas! I am saved alone." God help you, reader, to so receive and give, that you shall save yourself and others also.

> Must I go, and empty handed,
> Must I thus my Saviour meet,
> Not one soul with which to greet Him,
> Lay no trophy at His feet?

II.

CHRIST OUR SANCTIFIER.

And for their sakes I sanctify myself, that they also might be sanctified through the truth. John xvii: 19.

THE marginal reading of the last clause is, "That they also might be truly sanctified." This seems to imply that there is something which passes in the world for holiness, which is not true sanctification. There are counterfeit forms of Christian life, and also defective forms, which do not represent all that the fullness of Christ is able to do for us. Sanctification is the second step in the Four-fold Gospel.

I. WHAT IT IS NOT.

We will look at first what it is not. There are good elements and even holy elements in Christian character, which are not sanctification.

1. It is not regeneration. Sanctification is not conversion. It is a great and blessed thing to become a Christian. It is never a matter of small account. To be saved eternally is cause for eternal joy; but the soul must also enter into sanctification. They are not the same. Regeneration is the beginning. It

is the germ of the seed, but it is not the summer fullness of the plant. The heart has not yet gained entire victory over the old elements of sin. It is sometimes overcome by them. Regeneration is like building a house and having the work done well. Sanctification is having the owner come and dwell in it and fill it with gladness, and life, and beauty. Many Christians are converted and stop there. They do not go on to the fullness of their life in Christ, and so are in danger of losing what they already possess. Germany brought in the grand truth of justification by faith through the teachings of Martin Luther, but he failed to go on to the deeper teachings of the Christian life. What was the result? Germany to-day is cold and lifeless, and the very hot-bed of rationalism and all its attendant evils. How different it has been in England! The labors of men like Wesley, and Baxter, and Whitfield, who understood the mission of the Holy Spirit, have led the Christian life of England, and America, her offspring, into deeper and more permanent channels. You will find that the men and women who do not press on in their Christian experience to gain the fullness of their inheritance in Him, will often become cold and formal. The evil in their own heart will assert itself again and will be very likely to overcome them, and their work will bring confusion and disaster to the cause of Christ. If they escape the result, it will be as by fire. You have doubtless noticed young Christians who have seemed to be marvelously converted and filled with the love of God, but they have not entered into the deeper life of Christ, and in an evil hour they failed. They had gained a new heart, but they had neglected to get the deeper teaching and life which Christ has for all His children.

2. Sanctification is not morality, nor any attainments of character. There is very much that is lovely in human life which is not sanctification. A man cannot build up a good human character himself and then

call it the work of God. It will not stand the strain that is sure to come upon it. Only the house that is founded upon the Rock of Ages will abide securely in the wrath of the elements.

3. Sanctification is not your own work; it is not a gradual attainment which you can grow into by your own efforts. If you should be able to build such a structure yourself, and add to it year after year until it was completed, would you not then stand off with a pardonable pride and look upon it as your own work? No, dear friends, you cannot grow into sanctification. You will grow after you are in it into a fuller, riper and more mature development

of life in Christ, but you must take it at its commencement as a gift, not as a growth. It is an obtainment, not an attainment. You cannot sanctify yourselves. The only thing to do is to give yourself wholly to God, a voluntary sacrifice. This is intensely important. It is but a right thing to do for Him. But He must do the work of cleansing and filling.

4. Sanctification is not the work of death. It is strange that any one should think there could be a sanctifying influence in the dying struggle. Yet many have lived in that delusion for years. They expect that the cold sweat of that last hour and the convulsive throbbing of the

sinking heart will somehow place them in the arms of their Sanctifier. This comes in some degree from the old idea that their sin is seated in the body—the old Manichæan teaching that the flesh is unholy, and if we were once rid of the body, the fleshless tenant would be free from sin and would spring at once into boundless purity. There is no sin in these bones and flesh and ligaments. If you cast off your hand you have lost no sin. If both hands are gone you are as sinful as ever. If you cut off your head and yield up your life, sin would still remain in the soul. Sin is not in the body, it is in the heart, and the soul, and the will. Divest yourself of this body of clay, and the spirit will still be left, a hard, rebellious, sinful thing. Death will not sanctify it. It is a poor time to be converted. It will be a poorer time to be sanctified. I would not advise any one to put off their salvation to the dying hour, when the heart is oppressed and the brain clouded, and the mind has need of confidence and rest and a sense of victory to enable it to enter into His presence with fullness of joy. Nor is it a better time for the deeper work of the Holy Ghost. Sanctification should be entered into intelligent y when the mind is clear. It is a deliberate act calling for the calm exercise of all the faculties working under the controlling influence of the Divine Spirit.

5. Sanctification is not self-perfection. We shall never become so inherently good that there will be no possibility or temptation to sin. We shall never reach a place where we shall not need each moment to abide in Him. The instant we feel able to live without Him, there comes up a separate life within us which is not a sanctified life. The reason the exalted spirits in heaven fell from their high estate was, perhaps, because they became conscious of their own beauty, and pride arose in their hearts. They looked at themselves, and became as gods unto themselves. The moment you or I become conscious that we are strong or pure, that instant the work of disintegra-

tion begins. It has made us independent of Him, and we have separated ourselves from the life of Christ. We must be simple, empty vessels, open channels for His life to flow through. Then Christ's perfection will be made over to us. And we shall grow ever less and less in ourselves, as He becomes more and more within us.

6. Sanctification is not a state of emotion. It is not an ecstasy or a sensation. It resides in the will and purpose of life. It is a practical conformity of life and conduct to the will and character of God. The will must choose God. The purpose of the heart must be to yield to Him, to please and obey Him. That is the

important thing, to love, to choose and to do His holy will. You can not have that spirit in you and fail to be happy. The spirit that craves mere sensational joy has yet an unholy self life. It must get out of that form of self and i.to God before it can receive much from Him.

II. WHAT SANCTIFICATION IS.

Let us look at the positive side.

1. It is separation from sin that is the root idea of the word. The sanctified Christian is separated from sin, from an evil world, even from his own self, and from anything that would be a separating cause between him and Christ in the new life. It does not mean that sin and Satan are

to be destroyed. God does not yet bring the millennium, but He puts a line of demarcation between the sanctified soul and all that is unholy. The great trouble with Christians is they try to destroy evil. They think if sin could be really decapitated and Satan slain they would be supremely happy. It is a surprise to many of them after conversion that God still lets the devil live. He has nowhere promised that He will kill Satan, but He has promised to put a broad, deep Jordan between the Christian and sin. The only thing to do with it is to repudiate it and let it alone. There is sin enough in the world to destroy us all, if we take it in. The air is full of it, as the air in some of our Western States is full of soot from the soft coal that is burned there. It will be so to the end of time, but God means you and me, beloved, to be separated from it in our spirit.

2. Sanctification means also dedication to God. That is the root idea of the word also. It is separation from sin and dedication unto God. A sanctified Christian is wholly yielded to God to please Him in every particular; his first thought always is, "Thy will be done;" his one desire that he may please God and do His holy will. This is the thought expressed by the word consecration. In the Old Testament all things which were set apart to God were

called sanctified, even if there had been no sin in them before. The Tabernacle was sanctified; it had never sinned, but it was dedicated to God. In the same sense all the vessels of the Tabernacle were sanctified. They were set apart to a holy use. Dear friends, God expects something more of us than simply to be separated from sin. That is only negative goodness. He expects that we shall be wholly dedicated to Him, having it the supreme wish of our heart to love and honor and please Him. Are we fulfilling His expectations in this?

3. Sanctification includes conformity to the likeness of God. We are to be in His image, and stamped with the impress of Jesus Christ

4. Sanctification means conformity also to the will as well as the likeness of God. A sanctified Christian is submissive and obedient. He desires the Divine will above everything else in life as kinder and wiser for him than anything else can be. He is conscious that he misses something if he misses it. He knows it will promote his highest good far more than his own will, crying instinctively, "Thy will be done."

> " Thou sweet, beloved will of God,
> On thee I lay me down and rest,
> As babe upon its mother's breast."

5. Sanctification means love, supreme love to God and all mankind. This is the fulfilling of the law. It is the spring of all obedience, the

fountain from which all right things flow. We cannot be conformed to the image of God without love, for God is love. This is, perhaps, the strongest feature in a truly sanctified life. It clothes all the other virtues with softness and warmth. It takes the icy peaks of a cold and naked consecration and covers them with mosses and verdure. It sends bright sunlight into the heart, making everything warm and full of life, which would otherwise be cold and desolate. The savage was able to stand before his enemies and be cut to pieces with stoical firmness that disdained to cry, but his indifference was like some stony cliff. It was not the warm, tender love of the heart of Jesus, which made Him bow meekly to His painful death because it was His Father's will. It was the spontaneous, glad outflowing of His loving heart. Dear friends, if we are so filled with love to God, it will flow out to others, and we shall love our neighbors as we love ourselves.

III. THE SOURCE OF SANCTIFICATION.

The heart and soul of the whole matter is seeing that Jesus is Himself our sanctification. We must not look at it merely as some great mountain peak where He is standing and which we have to climb, but between us and it there are almost inaccessible cliffs to ascend before we can stand at His side. But Jesus

Himself becomes our sanctification. "For their sakes I sanctify myself, that they also may be truly sanctified." It seems as though He was a little afraid His followers would get to looking for sanctification apart from Himself, and knowing that it could never reach them except through Him, therefore He said, " I sanctify myself."

1. He has purchased it for us. It is part of the fruit of Calvary. By one offering He hath perfected forever them that are sanctified. "By the which will we are sanctified through the offering of the body of Jesus Christ once for all."

2. It does not come to us by our efforts, but it is made over to us as

the purchase of His death upon the cross. It is ours by the purchase of Jesus just as much as forgiveness is. You have as much right to be holy and sanctified as you have to be saved. You can go to God and claim it as your inheritance as much as you can your pardon for sin. If you do not have it you are falling short of your redemption privileges.

3. Sanctification is to be received as one of the free gifts God desires to bestow upon us. If it is not a gift then it is not a part of redemption. If it is a part of redemption, then it is as free as the blood of Jesus.

4. It comes through the personal indwelling of Jesus. He does not put righteousness into the heart

simply, but He comes there personally Himself to live. Words are weak; they, indeed, are utterly inadequate to express this thought. When we arrive at complete despair of all other ways we learn this truth. And Jesus Christ Himself comes into the heart and lives His own life there, and so becomes the sanctification of the soul. This is the meaning of the text. It is to His people that Jesus sanctifies Himself, and any who try to live a sanctified life apart from Him are not truly sanctified. They must take Jesus in as their life to be truly sanctified. That is the personal sense of divine holiness. "But of Him are ye in Christ Jesus, who of God is made unto us wisdom, and righteousness, and sanctification, and redemption." Jesus is made unto us of God wisdom. He is the true philosophy, the eternal *Sophia*, far above the deepest philosophy, righteousness, sanctification and redemption. So Jesus in our heart becomes our wisdom. He does not improve us, and make us something to be wondered at. But He just comes in us and lives as He did of old in His Galilean ministry.

When the tabernacle was finished the Holy Ghost came down and possessed it, and dwelt in a burning fire upon the ark of the covenant, between the cherubim. God lived there after it was dedicated to Him. So when we are dedicated to God, He comes to live in us and transfuses His life through all our being. He that came into Mary's breast, He that came down in power upon the disciples at Pentecost comes to you and me when we are fully dedicated to Him, as really as though we should see Him come fluttering down in visible form upon our shoulder. He comes from yonder world to live within us as truly as though we were visibly dwelling under His shadow. God does come to dwell in the heart and live His holy life within us. In the 36th of Ezekiel we have this promise: "I will sprinkle clean water upon you." That is forgiveness; old sins are all blotted out. "A new heart also will I give you;"

that is regeneration. "I will put My Spirit within you, and cause you to walk in My statutes, and ye shall keep My judgments and do them;" ah! that is something more than regeneration and forgiveness. It is the living God come to live in the new heart. It is the Holy Spirit dwelling in the heart of flesh that God has given, so that every movement, every thought, every intention, every desire of our whole being will be prompted by the springing life of God within. It is God manifest in the flesh again. This is the only true consummation of sanctification. Thus only can man enter completely into the life of holiness. As we are thus possessed by the Holy Spirit we are made partakers of the Divine nature. It is a sacred thing for any man or woman to enter into this relation with God. It places the humblest and most unattractive creature upon the throne with Him. If we know that God is thus dwelling within us, we will bow before the majesty of that sacred presence. We will not dare to profane it by sin. There will be a hush upon our hearts, and we will walk with bowed heads and conscious of the jewel we carry within our hearts. Do you know what it is to have Christ thus sanctified to you, beloved? Do you know personally what it is to be wholly dedicated to Him, and to hear Him say to you, "For your sake I sanctify myself that you may be truly sanctified?"

IV. HOW IT IS RECEIVED.

1. We must have a Divine revelation of our own need of sanctification before we will seek to obtain it. We must see for ourselves that we are not sanctified, and that we must be sanctified if we would be happy. The first thing God does often to bring us where we will see this, is to make us thoroughly ashamed of ourselves by letting us fall into mistakes and by bringing our frailties to our notice. In these humiliating self-revealings we are able to see where we are not righteous, and we are made to learn that we cannot keep our resolutions of amendment that we make in our own strength. God has let His dear

children learn this lesson all through the ages, and learn it by repeated failures, and each of us must ever learn it for himself.

2. We must come to see Jesus as our sanctifier. If with one breath we cry out, "O wretched man that I am! who shall deliver me from the body of this death?" with the next we must add, "I thank God through Jesus Christ, my Lord." We must see in Him that great deliverer, and know that He is able to meet our every need and supply it.

3. We must make an entire surrender to Him in everything. We must give ourselves to Him thoroughly, definitely and unconditionally, and have it graven in the heart, as if it

were written on the rocks, or painted on the sky. Cut it deeply in the annals of your recollection. Always remember that on that day and on that hour I gave myself fully to Christ and He became entirely mine.

4. We must believe that He receives the consecration we make. He is as earnest and as willing and as real about it as you are. Amid the hush of heaven He stoops to hear your vows, and He whispers when you have finished. "It is done. I will give to him of the fountain of the water of life freely. He that overcometh shall inherit all things."

Many people make a mistake about some of these steps. Some of them are clinging to a little of their old goodness and therefore meet with failures. Others stumble at the second step. They do not see that Jesus is their complete Sanctifier. And many cannot take the third step and make a complete surrender of everything to Him. Multitudes fail even when they have taken these steps in not being able to believe that Jesus receives them. Keep these four steps clear. "I am dead, my own life is surrendered and buried out of sight. Jesus is my Sanctifier and my all-in-all. I surrender everything into His hand for Him to do with as He thinks best. I believe He receives the dedication I make to Him. I believe He will be in me all I need in this life or in the world to come." I am certain, dear friends, when you have taken these four steps you can never be as you were before. Something has been done which can never be undone. You have become the Lord's. His presence has come into your heart; it may be like a little trickling spring upon the mountain side, but it will become great rivers of depth and power.

V. PRACTICAL STEPS

by which this life of sanctification is lived out day by day.

1. We are to live a life of implicit obedience to God, doing always what He bids and being henceforth wholly under His direction.

2. We are to be ever harkening diligently to His voice. We will need to listen closely, for Jesus speaks softly.

3. In every time of conflict or temptation or testing, we are to draw near to God and give the matter over to Him. Instead of the sweet and happy experiences you would naturally expect after such a consecration, the devil comes and tries to shake your confidence by some trial or temptation. Stand in Him and rejoice that He counts you worthy to receive such trials. If you fail, don't say it is no use to try further. The principle is right. Perhaps you tried to do the work yourself and so you failed. Stop and lay it all at His

feet and start afresh, and learn to abide in Him from your very failure. Israel, after their defeat at Ai, were stronger for the next conflict. Try to live out the secret you have learned. In human art there is always stumbling at first. You can learn the principles of stenography in a very little while, a few hours perhaps, but it takes months of patient practice to become expert at it. At one of our Western meetings recently, a lady was taking verbatim reports of the addresses. She was sitting at a little table with an instrument they call a stenograph. By touching the keys of this instrument a little needle cut impressions on a paper ribbon, representing with perfect accuracy the words that were spoken. She was able to learn the principle in a few hours, but it took many many more hours of quiet practice before she was so accustomed to it that she could do it easily. The moment we are consecrated to Jesus Christ we learn the secret that He is to be all-in-all to us. But when we try to practice this truth, we find that it takes time and patience to learn it thoroughly. We must learn to lean on Him. We must learn little by little how to take Him for every need. The principle is perfect. It will become absolutely unfailing in practice. Remember the secret of it is, "Without Me ye can do nothing." "I can do all things in Christ, who strengtheneth me."

III.

CHRIST OUR HEALER.

Himself took our infirmities and bare our sickness.—Matt. viii : 17. Jesus Christ the same yesterday, to-day and forever. Heb. xiii : 8.

I. WHAT DIVINE HEALING IS NOT.

WE WILL look at its negative side first. Wherever good is to be found a counterfeit of it also will soon appear. Any valuable coin is always imitated, and the great forger has been at work on this also. It is particularly necessary with this precious truth to guard against error.

1. Divine healing is not medical healing. It does not come to us through medicines, nor is it God's especial blessing on remedies and means. It is the direct power of the Almighty hand of God Himself. "HIMSELF took our infirmities," and He is able to carry them without man's help. We have nothing to say against the use of remedies so far as those are concerned who are not ready to trust their bodies fully to the Lord. For them it is well enough to use all the help that nature and science can give, and we cheerfully admit that their remedies have some value as far as they go. There is some power in man's attempts to stop the tides of evil that sweep over

a suffering world. But there comes a point in all efforts when we have to say, "Thus far shalt thou go and no further." Yet no one ought rashly to give up these human helps until they have got a better one. Unless they have been led to trust Christ entirely for something higher and stronger than their natural life, they had better stick to natural remedies. They need to be sure that God's Word distinctly presents healing for disease, and does it as definitely as it does forgiveness of sin.

2. Divine healing is not metaphysical healing. It is not a system of rationalism, which is taking on so many forms in the world to-day, like the chameleon, assuming the hue of

the surrounding foliage, according to the class of people it comes in contact with. What is commonly known as mind cure or Christian science, is one of the most familiar forms of metaphysical healing. In Chicago they call it the Science of Life, but it is practically the same thing. It puts knowledge and intellect, or the mind of man in the place of God. It is not healing by remedies, but by mental force. It is a system of false philosophy and a skeptical theology; a philosophy that is absurd and misleading, and a theology which is atheistic and infidel. The basis of it is, that the material world is not real. What seem to be facts are simply ideas. This church is only a circular idea in my brain, and you chance to have the same idea in yours, and so we call it a church ; but it is not, it is only an idea. As you sit there before me you are not there in tangible form, but I have an idea of you in my brain, as sitting there. I am not here either in any physical sense, but I, too, am an idea lodged in your mind. So the teachers of this error go on to say that there is no body. Disease, therefore, is not real because it has no basis to work on. If you accept this philosophy, the bottom will drop out of all disease. If the idea of sickness has gone from your mind, the trouble has gone. This is a frank, candid statement of the principles of this theory. It has captivated hundreds of thousands of people in this country and hundreds of thousands of dollars have been made out of it. It is the old philosophy of Hume revived again. The Bible is treated by these teachers in the same way as the body. It is a beautiful system of ideas, but they are only ideas. Genesis is a beautiful story of creation, but it is only an allegory. The New Testament contains a charming picture of Jesus Christ, but it, too, has no foundation in fact. It is the old errors that the Apostle John wrote strongly against. "Every spirit that confesseth not that Jesus Christ is come in the flesh, is not of God: and this is that spirit of Anti-Christ, where-of ye have heard that it should come; and even now already is it in the world." This philosophy denies that Jesus Christ has come in the flesh. It denies the reality of Christ's body; therefore, it is anti-Christism in its teaching. This is *not* Divine healing. There is no fellowship between the two. It is one of the delusions of science, falsely so called. It would undermine Christianity. Some of us have despised it so much that perhaps we have not guarded others against it as we should. We have felt it was so silly there could be no harm in it; but we forget how silly human nature is. The apostle tells us the wise in this world are fools with God. "He taketh the wise in their own craftiness." How truly this has been fulfilled in the case of New England! That land of colleges, the seat of American intelligence and culture, has given birth to this monstrosity. It is the most fatal infidelity. It does away entirely with the atonement, for as there is no sin there can be no redemption. I would rather be sick all my life with every form of physical torment, than be healed by such a lie.

3. Divine healing is not magnetic healing. It is not a mysterious current which flows into one body from another. It is a serious question whether there is such a force in nature as animal magnetism, and

whether what this seems to be, is not rather an influence to which one person's mind is subject from causes within itself. Whether this is so or not, the thought or claim of such an influence is repudiated by all who act as true ministers of Divine healing. Such a one is most anxious to keep his own personality out of the consciousness of the sufferer, and hold the eye of the invalid only on Christ, that he may take his healing from Him. There is nothing to be so much feared in this work as becoming the object of attention. It is heart to heart, and soul to soul contact with the living Christ, and with Him alone, that will accomplish the result.

4. Divine healing is not spiritualism. It cannot be denied that Satan has a certain power over the human body. Certainly he must have if he is able to possess it with disease. And, if he has power to inflict ill health upon the body, I see no reason why he should not, if he please, open the back door and get out and leave the body well. If Satan had power to bind a woman in Christ's time, for eighteen years, he had power to unbind her just as quickly. If sickness was his work then, it must surely be the same now. If he can use some persons better if they are strong and well, he will do so. Other instruments he can use better in weakness and pain. We cannot but

notice the strange persistency with which people of all ages have resorted to evil powers, either to appease them or enlist their help. The custom is as old as the earliest races. We find it with the wild Indian in the forest, and the equally savage African. Particularly have these wild incantations been performed for the healing of sickness, and it is said that many of them have actually resulted in the removal of the disease. There can be no question that great multitudes of spiritualistic phenomena are real. They give positive evidence of the reality of evil spirits, and they are proofs of God's terrible forewarning, that in the last days the spirits of devils shall be upon the earth working miracles, so that, if possible, they shall deceive the very elect. God's true child will not be deluded by them. If you are deceived about this thing, look out! You may not be God's true child. I warn you as you value your true welfare, avoid this seductive snare. You will find in it some reality, but it is a dangerous power and it will submerge your Christian faith beneath its hideous waves.

5. Divine healing is not prayer cure. There are many Christians who greatly desire others to pray for them. If they can secure a certain quantity of prayer there will come a corresponding influence for good

upon them, and if all the Christians in the world were to pray for them, they would expect to be healed. There is a general notion that there is a great deal of power in prayer which must have an effect if it can be concentrated. And if enough of it could be obtained, it would remove mountains and perhaps be able to break down God's stubborn will. This is practically what this view teaches. There is no power in prayer unless it is the prayer of God Himself. Unless you are in contact with Christ the living Healer, there is no healing. Christ's healing is by His own Divine touch. It is not prayer cure, but Christ-Healing.

6. Divine healing is not faith cure.

The term gives a wrong impression, and I am glad it has been discarded. There is danger of getting one's mind so concentrated on faith that it may come between the soul and God. You might as well expect your faith to heal you, as to attempt to drink from the handle of the chain pump with which you get fresh water, or to eat the tray upon which your dinner is brought. If you get to looking at your faith, you will lose the faith itself. It is God who heals always. The less we dwell on the prayers, the faith, or any of the means through which it comes, the more likely we will be to receive the blessing.

7. Divine healing is not will power.

No person can grapple with his own helplessness and turn it over into strength. It is a principle of mechanics that no body can move itself. There must be some power outside of itself to do this. Archimedes said he would be able to pry up the world if he could get some power outside of it to operate on it; but he could not do it from the inside. If man is down, all the power in his own soul will not avail to lift him up. The trouble too often is in his will. He tries to take hold of himself and lift himself up. He must have some power outside of himself to lift him, or he will remain down. The will must be yielded up to Christ, and then He will work in us to will and do of His good pleasure. Then the first thought will be how easy, how delightfully simple it is to receive the power from Him which we need. It is only touching God's hand and receiving strength from His life.

8. Divine healing is not defiance of God's will. It is not saying, "I will have this blessing whether He wills it or not." It is seeing that in having it we have His highest purpose for us. We will not trust for physical healing till we know it is God's will for us, then we can say, "I will it, because He wills it."

9. Neither is it physical immortality, but it is fullness of life until the life-work is done, and then receiving our complete resurrection life at the coming of Christ.

10. Divine healing is not a mercenary medical profession that men adopt as they would adopt a trade or profession in order to make something out of it. If you find the mercenary idea appearing in it for a moment, discountenance and repudiate it. All the gifts of God are as free as the blood of Calvary.

II. WHAT DIVINE HEALING IS.

1. It is the supernatural, Divine power of God, infused into human bodies, renewing their strength and replacing the weakness of suffering human frames by the life and power of God. It is a touch of the Divine omnipotence, and nothing short of it. It is the same power that raised

Jairus' daughter from the dead or converted your soul. Is it strange that God should show such power? More power is required to regenerate a lost soul than to raise the dead. God could shiver the sepulchre and bring out the forms of those who have lain there for years, with less expenditure of power than it costs Him to redeem one soul, and keep His saints steadfast unto the end.

2. It is founded, not on the reasoning of man, or the testimony of those who have been healed, but on the Word of God alone. All the testimony that could be gathered from the whole universe would not establish the truth of such a doctrine, if it is not to be found in the Scriptures.

All the deductions of the human intellect are worthless if they are not rooted there. This truth rests on God's eternal word, or it is merely human.

3. It ever recognizes the will of God, and bows to that in profound submission. A Christian who is looking for Divine healing will wait till he knows the will of God, and having learned that, he will claim it without wavering. If a sufferer is convinced that the work God gave him to do is done, and that now he is called home, then he should acquiesce in that will and lie down in those blessed arms and rest. If that conviction has come to any of you, dear friends, I would not dare to shake

you out of it, if you have been led into it by God. My only thought would be to sweetly smoothe your last pillow, and let you depart in peace. If, however, you think your work is not done, if you have not clear light from God that this is so, if there is a true and submissive desire in your heart to live and finish your course with joy, then He who said nearly two thousand years ago, "Ought not this woman to be loosed from this infirmity?" is the same today as He was then. He is saying to you in the midst of your weakness, "Ought you not to be made well?" Surely that should be enough.

It may be, however, that your sickness has been allowed to come as a discipline. You may have been holding back part of the full testimony or service Christ has called you to. I am afraid, then, you cannot be healed till that difficulty is made right. You may be in some wrong and crooked attitude. He probably will not restore you till that is adjusted. He may have called you to some service and you are holding back. There will not be healing for the body till you have yielded at this point. There are hundreds of meanings in the sicknesses that are allowed to come upon God's dear children, and He will show you what His voice is for you. "For God speaketh once, yea twice, yet man perceiveth it not. In a dream, in a vision of the night, when deep sleep falleth upon men in slumberings upon the bed, then He openeth the ears of men, and sealeth their instruction, that He may withdraw man from his purpose, and hide pride from man. He keepeth back his soul from the pit, and his life from perishing by the sword. He is chastened also with pain upon his bed, and the muititude of his bones with strong pain: so that his life abhorreth bread, and his soul dainty meat. His flesh is consumed away, that it cannot be seen; and his bones that were not seen, stick out. Yea, his soul draweth near unto the grave, and his life to the destroyers. If there be a messenger with him, an interpreter, one among a thousand, to show unto man his uprightness, then He is gracious unto him, and saith, 'Deliver him from going down to the pit: I have found a ransom.' His flesh shall be fresher than a child's; he shall return to the days of his youth." That is the meaning of many of God's chastenings. There is much that He would say to men through His dealings with their bodies, and it is necessary to get their full meaning into the soul before Divine healing can be received, and kept after it has been received. It is not a cast-iron patent that works inexorably in one way always; it requires a walk that is very close with God. When the soul is thus walking in harmony and obedience to Him, the life of God can fully flow into the body. Thank God, we cannot have it and have the devil, too.

3. Divine healing is part of the redemption work of Jesus Christ. It is one of the things He came to bring. Its foundation stone is the cross of Calvary. "He redeemeth thy life from destruction." "Deliver him from going down to death, I have found a ranson." Surely that healing comes from Himself alone. "By His stripes we are healed." That is the redemption work of Christ. You have a right to do it, beloved, for His body bore all the liability of your body on the cross.

Take it and love Him better, because it came from His stripes. I love to think of that word as being in the singular number, stripe. That is the Greek meaning. His body was so beaten that it was all one stripe. There was not an inch of His flesh but was lacerated for us. There is not a fibre of your body but Christ has suffered there to redeem it.

4. Divine healing comes to us through the life of Jesus Christ, who rose from the dead in His own body. He has gone up to heaven with His living body. You can see Him there this morning, with hands and feet of living flesh and bones, which you could handle. He could sit with you at the table and eat to-day as He did

of old. He is no shadowy cloud like form, but He has flesh and blood as we have. That is our Christ, a living physical Christ, and He is able and willing to share His physical life with you, by breathing into you His strength. We are healed by the life of Christ in our body. It is a tender union with Him; nearer than the bond of connubial oneness; so near that the very life of His veins is transfused into yours. That is Divine healing.

5. It is the work of the Holy Spirit, quickening the body. When Christ healed the sick while He was upon earth, it was not by the Deity that dwelt in His humanity. He said, "If I cast out devils by the Spirit of

God, then the Kingdom of God is come unto you." Jesus healed by the Holy Ghost. "The Spirit of the Lord is upon me, because He hath anointed me to preach the Gospel to the poor, to heal the broken hearts." The Holy Ghost is the agent, then, by which this great power is wrought. Especially should we expect to see His working in these days, because they are the days of His own Dispensation, the days in which it has been prophesied that there shall be signs and wonders. How did Samson receive his strength? When the Spirit of the Lord came upon him. Then he was able to hurl the temple into ruins and their god Dagon with it. The Spirit of God was in his flesh.

So when this electric fire is running through our frame, it brings healing and strength to every fibre.

6. Divine healing comes by the grace of God, not through the work of man. It cannot be bought, neither can it be worked for. We cannot help God out in it. We must take it as a gift. It comes to us as pardon does, a free gift from Him.

7. It comes to us by faith. It is not the faith that heals. God heals, but faith receives it. We believe that God is healing before any evidence is given. It is to be believed as a present reality, and then ventured on. We are to act as if it were already true. God wants us to lean on Him, and trust Him, and then re-

joice and praise Him for what He has given, with no doubt or fear.

8. Divine healing is in accordance with all the facts of Church history. From the time of Iræneus down to the present century there have been repeated examples of it. It is a long array, and great multitudes of healed ones proclaim with one voice : "Jesus Christ, the same yesterday, and to-day, and forever." All down through the middle ages the pure Church believed this truth and taught it. The Waldenses held it as an article of their faith. The times of the early Reformers are full of it. The lives of Luther and Baxter, and Fox and Whitfield, and John Wesley, give clear and convincing testimony that

they believed this truth. In later times the examples of it are numerous. Germany, Switzerland, Sweden, Norway, England and her colonies, and the mission fields of the world, have many witnesses to the healing power of Jesus. Our own land, and even our own city, are full of it. You have many witnesses to it here in your midst. You know them, and how some of them have stood the test of publicity and of years. They are not obscure cases. Many of them are men and women who have stood in the very front of Christian work. There is every kind of character and intelligence and temperament and disposition among them. There are children among them, as well as old men. Some of them have had lofty intellects, but they have been transformed into simple children. There are all classes of disease among them—from the terrible cancer to the most disordered of nervous organisms. And He has healed them all.

9. Divine healing is one of the signs of the age. It is the forerunner of Christ's coming. It is God's answer to the infidelity of to-day. Man may try to reason it down with the force of his intellect. God meets it with this unanswerable proof of His power.

III. HOW IS JESUS OUR HEALER?

1. Because He has brought healing for us with His stripes. It is a part

of His purchased redemption on Calvary. "Surely, He hath borne our sicknesses and carried our pains."

2. Because it is in His risen life in us. We have healing not only from Jesus, but in Jesus. It is in His living body, and we receive it as we abide in Him and keep it only as we abide in Him.

3. Because He enables us to take it by becoming our power to believe. He gives the faith to trust Him if we will receive it. We have not to climb the heights to find Him, but He comes down to our helplessness and becomes our trust as well as our healing. A Chinaman was once telling the difference between Christ and Confucius and Buddha. He said:

"I was down in a deep pit, half sunk in the mire and was crying for some one to help me out. As I looked up I saw a venerable, gray-haired man looking down at me. His countenance bore the marks of his pure and holy spirit. 'My son,' he said, 'this is a dreadful place.' 'Yes,' I said, 'I fell into it. Can't you help me out?' 'My son,' he said, 'I am Confucius. If you had read my books and followed what they taught, you never would have been here.' 'Yes, father,' I said, 'but can't you help me out?' As I looked up he was gone. Soon I saw another form approaching, and another man bent over me, this time with closed eyes and folded arms. He seemed to be looking into some far-off, distant place. 'My son,' he said, 'just close your eyes and fold your arms and forget all about yourself. Get into a state of perfect rest. Don't think about anything that could disturb. Get so still that nothing can move you. Then, my child, you will be in such delicious rest as I am. 'Yes, father,' I answered, 'I'll do that when I am above ground. Can't you help me out?' But Buddha, too, was gone. I was just beginning to sink into despair when I saw another figure above me, different from the others. He was very simple, and looked just like the rest of us, but there were the marks of suffering in His face. I cried out to Him: 'Oh,

Father, can you help me?' 'My child,' He said, 'what is the matter?' Before I could answer Him, He was down in the mire by my side; He folded his arms about me and lifted me up, and then He fed and rested me. When I was well, He did not say, 'Now, don't do that again,' but He said, 'We will walk on together now;' and we have been walking together until this day."

That's what Jesus Christ will do for you, beloved! He comes down to you where you are. He becomes your trust within you, and then you go on together until the resurrection light and glory of the coming age bursts in upon you. May God help us all to receive Him thus fully for His own name's sake! Amen.

IV.

CHRIST OUR COMING LORD.

I will give him the morning star. Rev. ii: 28.

THE SECOND COMING of the Lord Jesus Christ is a distinct and important part of the Apostolic Gospel. "I declare unto you the Gospel," Paul says to the Corinthians, and then begins to tell them of the Resurrection and the second Advent. It is, indeed, good news to all who love Him and mourn the sins and sorrows of a ruined world.

It is the glorious culmination of

all other parts of the Gospel. We have spoken of the Gospel of SALVATION, but Peter says our salvation is "ready to be revealed in the last time." Then only, when we stand amid the wreck of time and secure upon the Rock of Ages,

"Then, Lord, shall we fully know,
Not till then, how much we owe."

We have spoken of SANCTIFICATION, but John says: "When He shall appear, we shall be like Him, and every man that hath this hope in him purifieth himself, even as He is pure." And we have spoken of DIVINE HEALING, but Paul says: "God hath given us the 'EARNEST' of the resurrection in our bodies now," and Divine healing is but the first-springing life of which the resurrection will be the full fruition.

So that the truth and hope of the Lord's coming is linked with all truth and life, and is the Church's great and blessed hope. In the very beginning of human history God placed this great hope before His children. In the hour when man fell from Paradise, God erected in that fallen Eden, in the majestic figures of THE CHERUBIM, the prophecy and symbol of man's future glory. The faces of the lion, the ox, the man, and the eagle, were the types of the royalty, the strength, the wisdom, and the lofty elevation to which redeemed man was to rise in Jesus. These figures run through all the dispensations. They are God's portrait of His redeemed child after redemption's work is done. God sets before Himself and before man His sublime ideal for his future, and He will never rest till it is fulfilled. It is, therefore, well that besides the Gospel for the present, we should understand, and live under the power of THE GOSPEL OF THE FUTURE and the blessed and purifying hope of Christ's glorious coming.

I. WHAT WE MEAN BY CHRIST'S COMING.

1. We do not mean His coming to the individual Christian's heart. He does thus come most truly and graciously, and this is the blessed mys-

story of which we have already spoken in connection with our sanctification. It is "Christ in you, the hope of glory." But this is not His second coming. Some persons are ready to say, with a great show of spirituality, I have the millennium in my heart, and the Lord in my heart; let those who have not, speculate about a material coming. Well, Paul had the Lord in his heart, and a millennium as near to the third heaven as these persons will probably claim; and John was about as near his Redeemer's heart as any of us can ever expect to get on earth; but they did speak and write in terms like this: "Then we which are alive, and remain unto the coming of the Lord, shall be caught up in the clouds to meet the Lord in the air." "We know that when He shall appear, we shall appear with Him in glory." "Behold, He cometh with clouds, and every eye shall see Him. Even so, come, Lord Jesus."

Indeed, the more we know Jesus spiritually, the more will we long for His personal and eternal presence in the fuller and more glorious sense which His personal advent will bring.

2. We do not mean His coming at death. It is doubtful whether He does really come for us at death. Lazarus is represented as borne by angels into Abraham's bosom; and Stephen at his glorious departing

saw Jesus in heaven on the right hand of God, rising, it is true, to receive and honor his faithful servant, but not coming for him personally. The contrasts between death and the Lord's coming are very marked. We are not told to watch for death, but are delivered from its fear, but we are to watch for the Lord's coming. Death is an enemy; His coming a welcome visitation of our dearest friend. Death is a bitter bereavement to the heart; the Lord's coming is the very consolation of the bereaved, and the antidote of death. If death and the Lord's coming were identical, then the apostle would have said to the Thessalonian believers: "I would not have you ignorant concerning them that are asleep, that ye sorrow not as those that have no hope, for the Lord has come for them, and will soon in like manner come for you in death, and you shall be sweetly united in death once more." Does he say that? No! But he does say: "The Lord shall DESCEND FROM HEAVEN . . . and THE DEAD IN CHRIST SHALL RISE first, and then we that are alive shall be caught up together with them, to meet the Lord in the air, and so we shall be ever with the Lord." It is not death he points them to, but that which is to overcome death, and of which he says in writing to the Corinthians: "Then shall be brought to pass the saying that is written, 'Death is swallowed up in victory.'" If the Lord's coming is to swallow up death in victory, it is very certain that it cannot be the same thing, or it would swallow up itself.

3. We do not mean the spiritual coming of Christ through the spread of the Gospel and the progress of Christianity. This is nowhere recognized in the Bible as the personal coming of Christ.

"Behold, He cometh with clouds, and EVERY EYE SHALL SEE HIM, and they also which pierced Him, and ALL KINDREDS OF THE EARTH SHALL WAIL, BECAUSE OF HIM." Now, that is not the way they do when they receive the Gospel. They rejoice. But now they are startled and discouraged. And they cry, as represented in another place, to the rocks and the mountains to fall upon them and hide them from the wrath of the Lamb. So, also, the angels, speaking of this event to the eleven disciples, say: "This same Jesus SHALL SO COME IN LIKE MANNER AS YE HAVE SEEN HIM GO INTO HEAVEN." This cannot be the publication of the Gospel, but must be His PERSONAL, VISIBLE, AND GLORIOUS APPEARING. The Gospel is to be widely diffused; His truth is to prevail; His cause is to triumph, but He is coming personally, and He is infinitely more than even His truth and cause.

II. WHAT DO WE MEAN BY THE MILLENNIUM?

Some persons have stated that the doctrine of the millennium is a modern invention, and that the word itself is not found in the Bible.

The word millennium is not English, but is the Greek word for *a thousand years*. It is used repeatedly in the twentieth chapter of Revelation to denote the period during which Christ shall reign with His saints on the earth after the first resurrection. It is a time of victory, joy and glory. Seven especial facts are recorded concerning it here:

1. The resurrection and re-union of the saints.

2. Their reward and reign.

3. The complete exclusion of Satan from the earth.

4. The personal and continual presence of Jesus with them on earth.

5. The suppression of all enemies and the universal reign of righteousness.

6. The duration of a thousand years.

7. The immediately succeeding revolt of Satan and sinful man, and the final judgment of the wicked.

If there was no other reference in the Bible to this time of blessing, these elements alone would be sufficient to constitute a state and time of exalted glory and happiness. Much more do they suffice to identify it as the golden age of which former prophets wrote and spake, when righteousness, truth and peace shall " cover the earth as the waters cover the sea."

III. THE ORDER OF THESE TWO EVENTS.

This is the next question to be settled, and upon it hang most of the issues of the question. Is the coming of Christ to precede or follow this millennial period?

1. The most obvious reason for believing that it precedes it, is found in the very passage just referred to where these events are both described. There can be no question that here the coming of the Lord precedes and introduces the millennium. His coming is minutely de-

picted in the whole procession from heaven to earth. Then follows the conquest and punishment of His earthly foes, the binding of Satan, the resurrection of the saints, the reign of the risen ones and the thousand years. The only way it is attempted to set this aside is to represent it as figurative and spiritual. Dean Alford's strong sense and honesty is the best answer to this. If this be so, he declares, then adieu to all definiteness and certainty in the Scriptures. If this be not a literal coming, resurrection, and millennium, then we do not know what our Bibles mean about anything.

2. The next argument for Christ's premillennial coming, is the emphatic

use of the word, "WATCH," in connection with it. Many times are we told to watch for it. Now if it is to be preceded by a Spiritual millennium, the Lord would have told us to watch for this. How could the early Church watch for His coming, how can even we if we know that it is to be preceded by a clear thousand years? The very word watch means immanency, and it is not immanent, if ten whole centuries must intervene. If it be objected that as a matter of fact Christ's coming did not occur during more than ten centuries, this does not alter its immanency. An event may be liable to occur at any moment for years, and yet be long retarded. That is quite different from its being understood as not to occur until the later period. Although God knew just the moment when His Son should appear, yet He wanted His Church to be always expecting it—at even, or at midnight, or at cock crowing, or in the morning. The announcement of a fixed previous millennium would have been fatal to this design, and the Church would have gone to work to make her own millennium without Him. This is just what the Romish Church did, when Pope Hildebrand announced in the tenth century that the millennium had begun, and that Christ was already present through His vicar. And some Protestant teachers have the assumption to tell us to-day that this century of progress is the first age of the millennium.

3. The next proof of a premillennial coming is found in the picture Christ gives us of the condition of things as they were to be down to the close of the Christian age, and up to the very hour of His coming.

Just glance at a few bold touches in the picture.

Some seed fell by the wayside and the fowls of the air devoured them; some fell on stony places and perished; some were choked by thorns, and some fell on good ground and bore fruit.

But soon the enemy sowed the tares, and both grow together till the harvest.

The Church, externally, grows up into luxuriant strength like the mustard plant, but internally is full of leaven. The true and pure are like the hid treasure and the pearl, so hard to find. The net gathers of every kind and only the angels can separate the evil at the last.

As the ages roll on, there looms up the picture, not of a millennium, but a " Falling away first." " Wickedness shall abound and the love of many shall wax cold." " Many shall depart from the faith, giving heed to doctrines of devils." " In the last days perilous times shall come." There shall be plenty of church members, " having a form of godliness ; " but these shall be the very enemies of the Cross of Christ, "denying the power thereof." A holy, happy world will not be waiting to welcome its King, but "as a snare shall He come unto all that dwell on the earth." "When they shall say, 'Peace and safety, then sudden destruction.'" And when it bursts upon them, it shall find them "as it was in the days of Noah and of Lot;" and the Master even asks, "When the Son of man cometh, shall He find faith on the earth?"

This is God's picture of the future of earth until Christ's coming. It does not look much like a previous millennium.

No, nor does the story of eighteen centuries move towards a spiritual

millennium. New York with half
the proportion of church goers and
nearly double the ratio of drunkards,
has not grown any nearer to it in two
hundred years ; London, with three
million souls who never enter a
church ; Berlin, with one minister to
fifty thousand people ; these three
capitals of the three great Protestant
nations of earth hold out no signal of
its coming. And what shall we say
of wicked Paris, and rotten Constan-
tinople, and idolatrous India, and con-
servative China, and savage Africa ?
When is there coming to them as
much millennial light as we have ?
When will the Christian nation begin
to move toward their golden age ?
Oh, if this be the best God has for us,

then prophecy is an exaggeration and the Bible a poetic dream. Thank God, He is coming and His Kingdom shall transcend our brightest hope, and His own most glowing picture.

IV. OBJECTIONS.

The strongest objections that are made to this doctrine are :

1. It dishonors the work of the Holy Ghost, as if He were incompetent to fulfill His administration, and were represented as having failed in His great mission to convert the world, and some other means had had to be provided. In reply it is enough to say that the Holy Ghost has not undertaken to convert the world, but to call out of

it the Church of Christ and prepare a people for His name, and when this is done, and all who will accept Jesus as a Saviour have been called, converted and fully trained, the time for the next stage will have come, and Jesus will come to reign and restore His ancient people for their privileges and opportunities. The work of the Holy Ghost will not cease then, for He shall abide with us for ever, and the ages to come shall afford unbounded and more glorious scope for His grace and power.

2. It is objected that such a doctrine discourages Christian missions, and saps the foundations of the Church's most glorious hopes and

prospects. On the contrary, it opens a prospect of far grander glory to the Church at her Lord's appearing, and bids her go forth, rapt with the desire to hasten it, to prepare the world for His appearing; for as an incentive to this work, He Himself has told her that when the message of salvation has been proclaimed to all the world, then shall the end come. The fact is that a large majority of the missionaries now in foreign lands believe and rejoice in the blessed hope of the Lord's coming, are animated by it to labor for the world's evangelization, and cheered by the blessed thought that their task is not to convert the whole human race, but to evangelize the nations, and give every man a chance to be saved if he will ; and they would, indeed, be distracted and dismayed at the prospect they behold, did they feel that the world must wait until the present agencies have wrought out its full salvation, while meanwhile three times its entire population every century is swept into eternity unsaved. The coming of Christ is not going to suspend mission work. It will bring the most glorious and complete system of evangelization earth has ever seen. And under its benignant influence the heathen shall all be brought to Jesus ; all nations shall be blessed in Him, and all people shall call Him blessed. The most ardent friends of lost humanity must long the most for this, the world's best hope.

3. It is objected that this doctrine leads to fanaticism. Anything may be abused, but in the sober and Scriptural faith of this doctrine there is nothing fitted to minister to rashness, presumption or folly. Let us very carefully avoid all attempts to prophesy ourselves, or be wise above that which is written; but let us not be intimidated by the devil's howl, from the fullness of God's truth and testimony. This truth will make us a peculiar people. It will take away the charm of the world, and separate us from it. It will make us very unlike many selfish and comfortable

Christians, and will set our soul on fire to serve God and save men. And if that be fanaticism, then welcome such fanaticism.

4. It is objected that it is gross and material, tending to promote earthly and carnal hopes in the heart and the Church, like the earthly ideas and ambitions of the primitive apostles which the Master rebuked, and taught them rather to look for a spiritual kingdom and a heavenly home. That was the extreme then, may not the opposite be now? Is not the true need the spiritual first, afterward the material, the resurrection life of the soul first, then the resurrection of the body? We do not hold nor teach any gross or mate-

rial idea of the millennial age. The bodies of the saints will be spiritual, and like His own. But if He was pleased to take such a body into the heavenly world and make it the centre and crown of creation, is it anything but an affectation to try to be more spiritual than our Lord? Nay, it is all spiritual, and the true purpose and end of redemption is that "our whole spirit and soul and body be preserved blameless unto the coming of our Lord Jesus Christ," and "the whole *earth* be filled with His glory."

V. THE SIGNS OF HIS COMING.

While the day and the hour shall be unrevealed, yet His children "are not in darkness that that day should overtake them as a thief." "None, as the end approaches, none of the wicked shall understand, but the wise shall understand."

There is a distinct order revealed. He will first come for His own waiting ones, and they, with the holy dead, shall be caught up to meet Him in the air. The wicked world shall be left behind; a formal church and a multitude of nations shall live on and scarcely miss the little flock that has just been caught away. Then will begin a series of judgments and warnings, ending at last in the descent of Christ in power and glory, the revelation of His righteous judgment against His open enemies, and the beginning of

His personal reign. There will thus be two appearings of Jesus Christ—the one to His own, the other, later, to the entire world; the first as a Bridegroom, the second as a King and Judge. The signs of the one do not therefore apply to the other. The first of these appearings is not so sharply defined as the other. It is more immanent and uncertain, and may come at any hour.

Many of the most important signs of the Lord's coming have already been fulfilled. For example:

1. The political changes and developments of Daniel's great visions have apparently all occurred. The great empires have come and gone, and the minor kingdoms which were

to succeed them are now covering the regions which once they swayed.

2. The predicted "Falling away," has long ago begun, and the man of sin has sat in God's temple already the full time of the prophetic cycle, and the process has begun which is to "consume and destroy unto the end." The Papacy has fulfilled almost all the lineaments of its marvelous portrait.

3. The Mohammedan power has waxed and waned, and the waters of this great spiritual Euphrates are being dried up every day to prepare the way of God's kingly people.

4. The Jewish signs have not been less remarkable. Jacob is turning his face again to Bethel, and Jerusa-

lem is preparing to put on her beautiful garments again. Her sons are slowly gathering, while jealous nations are hastening the exodus, and fulfilling unconsciously the voice of prophecy.

5. The intellectual signs are not less marked. Knowledge is indeed increased and many run to and fro, while human philosophy talks of evolution and declares that all things continue as they were, and nature is immutable and only material.

6. The moral signs are even more marked than Daniel's picture. "The wicked shall do wickedly," was never more true than to-day. Portentous forms of wickedness startle the moral sense every day, and invention is as ripe in evil as it is in material art.

7. The religious signs are growing more vivid. Lukewarmness and worldliness in the Church, intense longings after holiness on the part of the few, and a mighty missionary movement are the features of the age, and the signs of prophecy, that point to the day of the Son of Man.

8. And finally, an earnest, a growing and a world-wide expectation of His coming on the part of all those who love His appearing, is as profound to-day as it was in Judea, and even the Gentile world in the age preceding His advent at Bethlehem. The morning star is in the East. "The children of the day" have seen it. The cry gone forth, "The night is far spent, the day is at hand;" and

soon the Sun will fill the sky and cover the earth with millennial glory.

VI. THE BLESSINGS OF HIS COMING.

1. It will bring us Jesus Himself. This is the best of its blessings. Like all the other sections of this Gospel, this, too, is the Gospel of Himself. Not the robes and the royal crowns, not the resurrection bodies or re-united friends will be the chief joy, but

> "Thou art coming, we shall see Thee,
> And be like Thee on that day."

2. It will bring us our friends. "Them who sleep in Jesus will God bring with Him." They shall be alive, they shall be recognized, they shall be gloriously beautiful, they

shall be ours forever. Not only the old ones, but such new ones, the good of all the ages, the men and women we have longed to know. What a family!

> "Ten thousand times ten thousand,
>   In shining garments bright,
> The armies of the ransomed
>   Throng up the steps of light;
> O then, what rapturous greetings
>   On Canaan's happy shore,
> What knitting severed friendships up,
>   Where partings are no more."

3. It will bring us perfect spirits, restored to His image, glorious in His likeness, free from fault, defect, or imperfection, removed above temptation, incapable of falling, and overflowing with unutterable blessedness. We shall wear His perfect image; we shall know as we are

known; we shall be as holy as He is holy; we shall possess His strength and beauty and perfect love. The universe will gaze upon us, and next to the glory of the Lamb will be the beauty of the bride.

4. We shall have perfect bodies; we shall possess His perfect resurrection life; we shall forget even what a pain was like; we shall spring into boundless strength; our hearts shall thrill with the fullness of immortal life, and space and distance be annihilated. The laws of gravitation will hold us no more. The streets of the New Jerusalem vertically and horizontally, the length and breadth, and the height thereof are equal. Our bodies shall be the perfect

instruments of our exalted spirits, the exact reflection of His glorious body.

5. It will give us the sweetest and highest service. It will be no idle, selfish ecstacy, but will bring a perfect partnership in His kingdom and administration. We shall, perhaps, be permitted to fulfill the ideals of our highest earthly experiences, and finish the work we have longed and tried to do—with boundless resources, infinite capabilities, unlimited scope and time, and His own presence and omnipotent help. The blessed work will be to serve Him, to bless others, and to raise earth and humanity to happiness, righteousness and Paradise restored.

6. It will banish Satan. It will bind and chain the foe and fiend, whose hate and power have held the world in ages of darkness and misery. Oh, to be free from his presence for even a day! to feel that we need no longer watch with ceaseless vigilance against him! to walk upon a world without a devil! Lord, hasten that glorious day.

7. And it will bring such blessings to others, to the race, to the world. It will stop the awful tragedy of sin and suffering; it will sheathe the sword, emancipate the captive, close the prison and the hospital, bind the devil and his henchman death, beautify and glorify the face of the earth, evangelize and convert the perishing

nations, and shed light and gladness on this dark scene of woe and wickedness.

>   There shall be no more crying,
>   There shall be no more pain,
>   There shall be no more dying,
>   There shall be no more stain.
>
>   Hearts that by death were riven,
>   Meet in eternal love;
>   Lives on the altar given
>   Rise to their crowns above.
>
>   Satan shall tempt us never,
>   Sin shall o'ercome no more,
>   Joy shall abide forever,
>   Sorrow and grief be o'er.
>
>   Jesus shall be our glory,
>   Jesus our heaven shall be;
>   Jesus shall be our story,
>   Jesus who died for me.
>
>   Hasten, sweet morn of gladness,
>   Hasten, dear Lord, we pray;
>   Finish this night of sadness,
>   Hasten the heavenly day.

Jesus is coming surely,
  Jesus is coming soon;
O let us walk so purely,
  O let us keep our crown

Jesus, our watch we are keeping,
  Longing for Thee to come;
Then shall be ended our night of
    weeping,
  Then we shall reach our home.

VII. THE LESSONS IT LEAVES.

1. Let us be ready. "The marriage of the Lamb is come and His wife hath made herself ready, and to her it was GRANTED that she should be arrayed in fine raiment, clean and white." Thank God that the robes are *given*. Let us have them on. WHITE ROBES. When the Bride is dressed, the wedding must be near. So let us hasten His coming.

2. Let us be watching. "Behold,

I come as a thief ; blessed is he that watcheth and *keepeth his garments,* lest he walk naked and they see his shame." Let us not put off the wedding robe for an hour. Let us remember His words, "When these things begin to come to pass, then lift up your heads and bend YOURSELVES BACK (Dr. Young), for your redemption draweth nigh." Keep your faces turned heavenwards until your whole being shall curve heavenwards, like a dear, old colored saint we know, whose body, when she speaks and prays, describes a circle bending towards the sky.

3. Be faithful. It is to bring the reward of faithful servants. Let us "look to it that we lose none of the

things which we have wrought, but may receive a full reward." "Hold fast that thou hast that no man takes thy crown."

In the ancient Church there was a noble band of forty faithful soldiers in one of the Roman legions, who were condemned to die for their faith in Jesus. They were all exposed on the centre of a frozen lake, to perish on the ice, but allowed the choice of recanting from their faith at any moment during the fatal night by walking to the shore and reporting to the officer on duty.

As the night wore on the sentinel on shore saw a cloud of angels hovering over the place the martyrs stood, and as one by one they dropped, they placed a crown upon the martyr's brow and bore him up to the skies, while all the air rang with the song, " Forty Martyrs and Forty Crowns." At last they had all gone but one, and his crown still hung in the sky above and no one seemed to claim it. Suddenly the sentinel heard a step, and lo! one of the forty was at his side. He had fled. The sentinel looked at him as he took down his name, and then said: " Fool, had you seen what I have seen this night you would not have lost your crown. But it shall not be lost. Take my place, and I will gladly take yours ; " and forth he marched to death and glory, while again the silent choir took up the chorus, " Forty Martyrs and

Forty Crowns. Thou hast been faithful unto death and thou shalt receive a crown of life."

God help us to hear that chorus when He shall come!

4. Be diligent. There is much to do. You can "hasten the coming of the day of God." The world is to be forewarned. The Church is to be prepared. Arouse thee, O Christian. Give Him every power, every faculty every dollar, every moment. Send the Gospel abroad. Go yourself if you can. If you cannot, send you substitute. And may this last decade of the nineteenth century mean for you and for this world, as nothing ever meant before, a time of preparation for the coming of our Lord and Saviour Jesus Christ!

www.ingramcontent.com/pod-product-compliance
Lightning Source LLC
Chambersburg PA
CBHW030340170426
43202CB00010B/1190